TEN BURNT OFFERINGS

By the same author

★

OUT OF THE PICTURE
THE EARTH COMPELS
AUTUMN JOURNAL
PLANT AND PHANTOM
SELECTED POEMS
CHRISTOPHER COLUMBUS
SPRINGBOARD: POEMS 1941-1944
THE DARK TOWER AND OTHER RADIO SCRIPTS
HOLES IN THE SKY
COLLECTED POEMS, 1925-1948

★

Translations
AGAMEMNON OF AESCHYLUS
GOETHE'S FAUST

TEN
BURNT
OFFERINGS

by

LOUIS MACNEICE

New York

OXFORD UNIVERSITY PRESS

1953

Every voyage is a death,
Every action is a loss,
Every poem drees its weird,
Carries its meaning like a cross;
Yet the burnt poet loves the fire
Which gulps what pittance he can giv —
Dry words dying, dying, dead,
Burning that the Word may live.

MAYDAY 1951

CONTENTS

These ten poems were written in Greece between March 1950 and April 1951 and are printed here in the order in which they were written.

Some of them appeared previously in *The New Statesman and Nation*, *World Review*, and *Botteghe Oscure*, and some had already been broadcast by the B.B.C.

I

SUITE FOR RECORDERS

... it strikes a man more dead than a great reckoning in a little room.

AS YOU LIKE IT

I

If shepherd to nymph were the whole story
Dying in holocausts of blossom,
No midwife and no middleman
Would contravene the upright sun.

If Raleigh to Marlowe on the other
Hand were an uncontested audit,
Then Thames need only flow to mock
A death in tavern or on block;

Nor swimming Hellespont nor climbing
Starwards could answer the inquiring
Blade that would spill each threaded bead,
Each grace-note of a broken reed;

While far sou'wested Eldorado,
Old pipe-dream in the Tower of London,
Would be no more than history claims—
A long axe handle spliced for James.

But if—that If!—to die while swearing
Be lambing time and back to living
They leap the gap, some black, some white—
What matter so the heart be right?

13

They leap the gap, these pets of northern
Adventurers in their idler moments,
And call from arrogant eyes and mouth
A smile to greet a borrowed South,

Where close-cropped vines, though but black fingers,
Cock snooks at time, acre on acre
Proclaiming with a million Ayes
The long-dead shepherd worth his prize.

And though Black Jenny spin her coarsest
Pall on Persepolis and Mayday,
Though Time drive ships from sail to steam,
Though what was vision shrink to dream,

Yet Thames flows on beneath the traitors'
Bodiless heads and Spenser's carefree
Swans are found loyal to their creed
That deathbed comforts bridal bed.

Great reckonings come, yet cheat nor schemer
Outlives, outdies, his early beauty,
Black fingers will bear fruit and spring
Put paid to every reckoning.

II

In a little room, a little plot, a little lifetime,
Hark, the shrill recorders after meat; the Elizabethan
Mayflies in a silver web which dangled over chaos,
    Twirling round and round,
Waited for the silent headsman, countering his silence
    With arabesques of sound.

Courtier with the knife behind the smile, ecclesiastic
With faggots in his eyes, tight-lipped scholar with forbidden
Fruit in his back garden, all were conscious in their bowels
    Of the web and whose it was
And beneath it of the void where not old faith nor yet new
       learning
    Dare breathe the word Because.

Chancing, dancing, in the threads of life, time, death, at least of
  something,
Though always over nothing, Spanish gold, high ruffs, carved
  crossbones,
All were solid—like stage props—to men and women only
  players,
    Only women, only men,
Briefed to make one first if last appearance more or less word-
  perfect,
    Having no chance again.

Golden age? Age of discovery? Age of madrigals and liars,
Age when men died young. We envy what we think an
  innocent ardour,
What in fact was staged revolt upon a tightrope, a creative
    Despair, a blithe despair of youth,
Which in that swivelling dubious web essayed its white lies in
  defiance
    Of the black void of truth.

Violent men with salt in their nostrils, blood on their hands,
  whose gentler moments
Conjured up, for lack of sleep, a land which ancient literati,
Careless of the starved and sweaty facts, had filled with mimic
    Shepherds fluting to their sheep
For Spenser, Sidney, Kit and Will to loll and count and then
  recounting
    Their antics fall asleep.

Life as a game? An art? An orgy? Something of each; a
  mortification
Also. Prematurely dead—or dumb—they left behind them
What for us? A bed of flowers? A second best? A starting
  point? Or
  Blind end, blind spring, spring of a trap?
Yet still they pipe and still from No Man's Pastures trip their
  white, their ringstraked,
  Their black sheep through the gap.

III

Pride in your history is pride
In living what your fathers died,
Is pride in taking your own pulse
And counting in you someone else.

Which someone, though long dead before,
Scrabbles and chirps on your own floor;
The orange he can hardly hold
Contains a world of Spanish gold.

Members one of another? Who
Could prove by reason that gag true?
But reason, if it were a lie,
Should counsel us at once to die.

For pride in being alive is what?
Is being what yourself are not,
Is being a world which must outlive
All you take from it or give.

Your Alter Egos, present, past,
Or future even, could not last
Did your word only prove them true;
Though you choose them, yet they chose you.

In and of the world and yet
Distinct from it, our task is set
To become Atlas while we can
And bear the world which made us man.

The windblown web in which we live
Presumes a yawning negative,
A nothing which cries out to see
A something flout its vacancy.

To singe the beard of the King of Spain
Was but a token; Tamburlaine
Found no more in his earthly crown
Than was allowed to Corydon;

And both demanded something more
Than their set piece of love or war,
Than what faint echoes drift to us
Of muffled drums or calamus.

Yet read between those lines and peer
Down through the mesh of gossamer
And you will sense the darkness which
Made either guttering candle rich;

And you, a would-be player too,
Will give those angry ghosts their due
Who threw their voices far as doom
Greatly in a little room.

IV

Come, my sheep, my goats, graze where the shoots are tender,
    Now I will sing of her
Who passed but once this way and never again till Judgment
    Day become Mayday too
And ribbons are round the Cross. Come where the grass is
    emerald;
    Battles were fought here once.

Come, my flocks, but shun the rusty wire, the tank-traps;
    Now I will sing of her
Whose shadow was taller than she and never till shadows have
    voices
    Dare I expect a reply
To the song I sung to her once. But come while the shadows
    lengthen,
    Graze your fill before night.

Come, this pipe is only on loan, I only a hireling,
    Yet, though my hire be due
And always unpaid, and my songs, heard by you only,
    Must needs be always unheard,
Come, my flocks, where this twilit wall still holds the noon-
    heat;
    Now I will sing of Her.

II

AREOPAGUS

I

A tall story over a dark sanctum:
That Hebrew riddling in a land of olives
    Was an appetiser for a tired mind.
With a stone in it too. A sharp titillation
    With a snub, if not threat, in it too.

Never built on, not then nor since.
The saint on the run had a sword in his mouth
    And his feet on the rock were rock;
Iron faith in the city of irony.
    As it were scales had dropped in Damascus.

Outcrop of judgement. The foreign accent
Souring their salt. Beneath in the cave,
    Once avenging, later beneficent,
With tousled vipers, gravestone eyes,
    The Kind Ones turned in their sleep.

Limestone burning the feet, and opposite
Tiers of Pentelic, he whetted the blade
    Of the wit of his faith to slice their pagan
Prides to the quick; they nudged and doubted.
    Diamond cut diamond. Something new.

II

Spermologies fallen on stony ground. Stone of relentlessness,
    stone of crime,
Where hard words flew in the dark. Primaeval
Echoes of evil. A nuance, a noise,
As of Titans gurgling into the sink of the world.

21

And the torches hissed where now, ringed round with
    mountains,
Flow seas of electric light. New lamps for old;
Red eggs for Easter. Stones are rolled away
And caves are fallen in; yet raise your eyes
From these children with old faces, from these women
With handkerchiefs over their faces, from these hands
Which decimate time with beads, you still may glimpse
The child-eyed Fury tossing her shock of snakes,
Careering over the Parthenon's ruined play-pen.

Old testaments for new. New blood for old.
If Christ be beyond us They can be grasped who grasp;
We each have inherited curses and breed our own and not all
The gadarene jeeps nor all the taverna bouzoukis
Can utterly drown the pack that yelps on the scent.

Ech! Ech! Ooh! Ech! Ech! Oo-o-oh!
Hide if you choose in Stoa and Garden,
Your own crisp words will begin to hiss
In key with our torches, in step with our snakes,
And your own sharp eyes, at home to doubt,
Will blur with a greater despair: belief.

Ech! Ech! Ooh! Which is why Paul
Scouring the market found an altar
Clearly inscribed but between the words
Was the ghost of a Word who runs may guess,
Who runs from a fate unclear, unkind.

Unkind was early, clear was classic,
Now it was late. But for Paul was early
And the trumpet about to sound; the Virgin
Mother was one more daughter of Night,
She and her son not yet scaled down
To ikon or niche; like those other Virgins
Long brought down to classical earth.

Down to life-size. Poet and builder
Paid off the Avengers. Then came Christ
Speaking a sword that was red from his own
Lungs and his arms sprawled on the cross
To strangle the world; till bishop and builder
Gilded the nails, adjourned the verdict,
And boxed the cross in a square.

No nonsense for Pericles—nor for Byzantium;
The shapeless shapes were a whiff of the past
And the whale-mouthed arch the bones of the future,
So the words of Paul were swamped in rock
To hiss like the snakes that hissed in their sleep
On the heads of the sleepers, daughters of Night,
Drowned, disregarded, thought of as nonsense.

And yet not utterly. No long walls
Put out and cut off like feelers, no stings drawn,
No schools of rhetoric or resignation,
Not fez and hookah (there is no God but God),
Not tommy-gun and brochure (there is no god but Man),
Could cancel out Christ's death or prove the Furies dead.
Scale from the beam, beam from the eye, scales from the eye had
        dropped in Damascus
For a trap had snapped in a flash on a lonely dust-white road
While in a limestone cave the past was not dead but sleeping.

III

After anemones, after almond,
Pitiless heaven, enamelled sea;
The Furies plumped the grapes with blood,
Their living rock was the death of sea.
As Christ's dead timber fired by blood
Was to blossom bright as peach or almond.

The Unknown God? Judge or saviour?
The unknown goddesses—Cursing or kind?
Shall we have neither? Either? Both?
The dark prehistory of their kind
Hung over Jews and Greeks and both
Found, of their kind, a likely saviour.

Christ, if we could, having Christian fathers;
But Furies, if we must. For no
Life is for nothing, all must pay,
Yet what unknown is dread, we know
Can yet prove kind; our selves can pay
Our sons atonement for their fathers.

After the murder, after the trial,
Justice undone but honours new,
Who came to blight had stayed to bless
This folk; old fears were born anew
As hopes, and flock and crop could bless
The powers that put man's faith on trial.

The fierce pack bays no more; their note is new.

IV

Flying and ravening Curses, bark no more!
The blood of all the world lies doubtless at our door
But at whose not? These questions have been bruited, solved,
     unsolved before.

His mother's keeper? Leda brought to bed
Could have heard you even then, distantly howling; your red
Torches formed an early canopy over her grandson's head.

But, Saul called Paul, adjourn your day of doom.
Orestes too was acquitted. The body may be a tomb
Yet even the beggar's body is bread, is wine, is flowers in bloom;

Trundle back then that weight of sin from the grave.
With the cross hidden in the square, the Furies hidden in the
    cave
Ripening the corn, Christ too must have bodies too to save.

Nightmares are often just. This starlit court
None the less cut one just, one divine, impeachment short;
The plaintiffs foiled of blood emerged of fair, not ill, report—

Venerable ripeners of crop and flock,
Smiling on yeoman and bride, warding off blight and shock,
They made their haven for good beneath this judicial, this
    grim, rock.

Could we too lead our Furies to their shrine?
Forget them sprung from blood, remember them divine?
Nurses of fear and hope, come taste our honey, taste our wine!

III

COCK O' THE NORTH

But I am half a Scot by birth, and bred
A whole one, and my heart flies to my head . . .
DON JUAN

I

Bad Lord Byron went to the firing, helmet and dogs and all,
He rode and he swam and he swam and he rode but now he
    rode for a fall;
Twang the lyre and rattle the lexicon, Marathon, Harrow and
    all,
Lame George Gordon broke the cordon, nobody broke his fall;
Mavrocordato, Colocotroni, faction, fiction and all,
All good fellows in fustanellas but all good fellows must fall.
Fall, fall, the kodjabashis! Snuff, douse, the Turkish moon!
Dollar credits with Barff and Hancock, conches in the sick
    lagoon!
Don John had fought Lepanto, Don Juan will dare it too;
Knaves and slaves are burning Sappho—hubble-bubble,
    hullabaloo!
'Flies and lice and fleas and thieves', Jeremy Bentham and gin—
Scusi! Scusi! Entusymusy! How did I ever get in?
In amidst this waste of marshes, waste of muskets, waste of
    breath,
In with the rogues, the cranks, the pirates, in and under, in at
    the death.
    The Pilgrim came down like a wolf in the cold,
        Kept from the door and trapped in the limelight,
    His tartan was faded, his nerves were old,
        But he knew a hawk from a handshake.

Pepper trees drooping and mist on the swamp—
    Oh Meleager! Ah Meleager!
Where is Leonidas? Has he struck camp?
    Where is my shield to be borne on?
Hail, hail, the conquering hero! Flaunt, vaunt, the hoplite's
    purse!
Rain on the roof and mud in the blood but everything might be
    worse.
The London Committee drool in the City, Castlereagh turns
    to curse,
While we are deficient in men and munitions, still everything
    might be worse.
Worse, worse, than stench and vermin, worse, worse, than
    sugary lies,
'Speculators and peculators'; Miltiades is coming,
The golden age is coming back, coming to life the poppied
    eyes,
Spring and Greece and glory—and Easter too—are coming.
    Easter is coming and the guns will boom:
        Christos anéste! Christos anéste!
    Scarlet flowers from a far-off tomb,
        Christos! Christos anéste!

II

The flattest place, it seems, in Hellas. A bad dream
The sea gets never deeper, nor is it sea;
A thin mud line coalesces with the horizon.
Whose name was writ in bilge . . . A stilted hovel
Like a sick bird stood hunched in the lagoon,
Its thatchy feathers moulting. Stepping stones through pus
But the next step was where? Across the gulf
The mountains of the Morea seemed a mirage; to the east
What there remained of a river flowing from Calydon

Wept stones for Meleager. The boar was black
Like the after-life of an Ethiop; his tusks
Flashed curving through the forest like the Milky Way
And his small eyes were death. But not Meleager's;
His death came through fire, in his hour of triumph,
Through a fire some miles away. And miles behind, away,
Byron while shooting duck felt groping at his liver
The flames in Six Mile Bottom. You would never guess
This from his statue in the Garden of Heroes
Among the arranged trees and the marble clichés
And the small memorial cannon like staring infants
With lollipops in their mouths. You would never guess
From Greece who Veeron was. Across the gulf—
'*Hier stand, hier sass* Their Royal Highnesses . . '
The marble bust of Clauss, benevolent distiller,
Guards his titanic vats, German epigonos
Who found Greece free and under a foreign king,
Frockcoats instead of turbans. Now in the heat
Missolonghi yawns and cannot close its mouth
And all its bad teeth show. The tired horizon
Remains a line of mud. In the plain around
The fruit trees, like his Souliots, wear white stockings,
The oleanders are pink and dry beside the river
Which weeps for Meleager. Crackle and hiss
On the hearths of Calydon and Kirkby Mallory.
Who had faced the brute, his life in the log—
But so far away—was burning away.

III

Close the vein! It is Easter Eve.
The long white candles wait to be lit,
The staring guns are agog to boom,
The boar is dark in the night of the wood,

The boar is dead in the glens of myth,
There is only a flame in the back of the mind
Consuming a log, the soft grey ash
Soft as, not grey as, the locks of hair
He hoarded in drawers. Close the vein!

Bruno and Millingen, close the vein!
The leech is black on the pale of the brow;
Poor me, poor Greece, there is my life to her!
My windows are misted within and without
Above the lagoon neither deep nor rolling;
Is this Greece Greece and is that sea sea
And what is there dear in the world? Adonis
He too went hunting boar and died
But the goddess loved him. Adonis *anéste*!

Afraid of the dark? Come and take light,
Where is your candle? I have no candle,
Only a sword. Which I have not used.

IV

Bards wha hae for Hellas bled—
  Oh Meleager, ah Meleager—
Anemones flourin' frae your blude
  When twa white queens focht owre ye!
Christ is wax, Adonis wax—
  Oh Cythereia, ah Cythereia!
The dumb tongues o' the candle wicks
  Haud ne'er a hint o' harvest.
A far cry here frae Aberdeen—
  Mither! Mither! Wae the Gordons!
Yon granite tours cam clatterin' doun
  I' the sunset waves o' Zante.

A far cry here frae Melbourne House—
   Dice in Almack's, flames in Moscow—
I' the year o' the stockin'-frame and waltz
   Wi' the price o' bread still risin'.
A far cry here frae the Grand Canal!
   That which once was! Breasts and eyebrows!
The vein is closed and the profit nil
   And the rest is Barff and Hancock.
The rest is a nicht where nae rest is—
   Oh Missolonghi, ah Missolonghi!
The dogs i' the nicht are ill at ease
   For they snuff the boar i' the reed-banks.
His white tusks curve like a Turkish sword—
   Back to the nightmare! Back to the nursery!
Our Lady o' Death has all assured
   And her board is spread for Adonis.
The dried branch is itchin' to bloom—
   Mither! Mither! *Crede Biron!*
Was it my fault you bore me lame
   To a warld o' sharks and dandies?
To thae bricht lichts where licht is nane?
   Christ gies licht but nae to pagans!
I maun burn my body to clear my een,
   Yon withered bough maun blossom.
To fell yon boar means death by fire—
   Calydon saved and Calydon ruined,
But the flame o' courage feeds on fear
   And the halt mak lordly riders.
Qu'allais-je faire dans cette galère?
   Was it for her sake, was it for my sake,
I flew like a bumblin' moth to the lure
   O' the gutterin' lamp o' Hellas?
Open the vein, I maun gie her oil,
   Oil from my guts an' oil from my marrow;
Yon leech is black as a ganglin' eel

c
      33

I' the dour lagoons beneath me.
Yon boar is black as the nicht o' the heart
    Wha bides my shaft and bodes my passin';
I maun gang my lane to wed my hurt,
    I maun gang my lane to Hades.
The fire is low in Calydon hall—
    Mither! Mither! Blaw the bellows!
My foreign doctors kill to heal
    And the last licht leads to darkness.
Under the bed, look under the bed,
    What is it growlin', what is it groanin'?
Thunder at sunset! What can it bode?
    Is it mysel'? My sunset?
You may throw my brand in yonder fire—
    Oh Meleager! *Crede Biron!*
I will hae the courage o' my fear
    And blaze a path to silence.

IV

DIDYMUS

I

A million simmering kettles: in the Destroyer's shrine
The world is on the boil, bats in malodorous dark
Under a pyramid of writhing sculpture
That rams the destroying sky. But round the unsculptured
    lingam,
The restful purposeful indifferent phallus,
The bats like microbes stitch their hectic zigzag
Of black on black, of blind on blind, and dot
And carry and dot and carry and sizzle like seaweed
That reeks on the shore of the Infinite. While outside
The whole of India jinks and twitters too
Around her granite axis; so shrill yet so resigned,
Monochrome under her motley, monolith under her flimflams.
Mute column of black stone hung round with grace-notes.
Smoke from no visible fire; yet fire like a fir-cone
Nestles in Shiva's hand, the dainty embryo
Of all that is and the end of all, the core
That never moves nor melts yet holds the dance,
Innumerable limbs reduced to one
Black pencil of pure fire. Roses and sandalwood,
Red spittle on the flagstones of the temple,
Green flash of parrots, phosphorescent waves,
Caparisoned elephants and sacred bulls,
Crystal-gazers, navel-gazers, pedants,
Dazzling and jangling dancers, dazzling lepers,
Begging unfingered hands and mouthing eyes,
Faces on faces each like a blind end,
Lives upon lives bubbles of jewelled scum

Born every second and reborn regardless,
Who has come here against you? Slow of speech
With trouble in his eyes and tarry hands
And no sophistication and no caste,
Who has come here armed with two plain crossed sticks
To flout your banyan riot of dialectic?
Is it a prince whose veins run blue with magic?
Is it a sage whose water-divining mind
Will twitch to the smallest drop at the final nadir?
Is it a god who has more arms than yours,
More words, more shapes, more worlds, invincible avatar?
No; it is Doubting Thomas.

II

Nothing more simple. Among the tarnished
Mirrors of paddy and cocoanut palms,
Black-and-white turkeys in courtly fantails,
And no human beings but children,

Tiny and self-assured in whitewash
Stands a plain church, no frills, no gilt,
Among Portuguese names on wooden crosses,
The Church of the Little Mount;

Whitewashed also within—the barrel
Vault as hale as a barrel of flour.
But under the chancel there sleeps a crypt
Not so much crypt as cave;

And here, says the plaque, here in Madras
Before Madras or madeira was heard of
Here was the hiding place of the saint
Who had left his faith to his hands.

His two hands only, only two—
What could they prove against Shiva and Krishna?
Or against the sweet-toothed jumbo-god
With his trunk in the bowl of candy.

Peter would have talked big and John
Have called forth a serpent out of the sherbet,
Paul would have matched them abstract with abstract
But this man, how could he start?

With his two hands and his cruse of doubt
Which never ran dry? And even doubting,
For those dark and sly and chameleon minds,
Was a technique they knew.

So, after days in the cave, of a night
He would sneak to the beach and watch the indifferent
Waves of the shark-ridden ocean and dream
Of nets that he used to mend

And of the man who spied him at it;
He could no longer remember his face
Nor most of his words, he could only remember
That his nets were repaired on time

And that so it began, a doubtful beginning,
His fisherman's hands were hardly right
For a preacher's gestures, he would have sooner
Saved them to tie strong knots.

Yet, staring out at the phosphorous wave-tops
And brushing away the eye-flies, Thomas
Thought of the Indian kings who never
Would raise a hand, having hands

39

Bought by the thousand for them, slaves
With enormous fly-whisks; and Thomas thought
Of the Indian gods who could sprout at pleasure
All the hands they might need.

And then he thought: I am proud, I have only
Two hands for all things, including the cross,
As have the coolies; it is my mission
To help their lack with mine.

And beside that sea like a sea on the moon
He clasped his hands to make sure they were only
Two and, finding them two but strong,
Raised them gently and prayed.

III

Oh but my doubt is a sea harsher than this that I see,
    Oh but my hands tremble fumbling the night,
To all of my questions I know the reply must be No;
    To me those tongues of fire were fire, not light.

Blessed are those who believe and ask no leave
    Of hand or eye, for whom all water is wine,
Who whatever the weight on the heart have the heart to wait
    For the clouds to lift—a gift that was never mine.

Whatever the clime, my task is ever to climb
    Foothills that never are mountains; this Indian sky
Is bowed with the dour monsoon and I doubt but soon
    All of my converts and most of my work must die.

I doubt that I have the least right to preach or write
    In the name of Christ, I doubt that my doubt can find
One hint that my terrible role could aspire to roll
    The stone from the door of the tomb of the Indian mind.

I doubt and I doubt; in a crumbling exposed redoubt,
    Enfiladed by heathendom, here to the end
I watch in the endless rain to herald the reign
    Of the Friend of Man—but can he be Thomas's friend?

Was he that once, the sole delight of my soul?
    My memory wilts in the heat. I was mending a net
When I sensed with a start that I was under his eye
    And he called my name; the rest of his words I forget.

Is he my friend still? No, perhaps. All that I know
    Is that each rice-farmer, snake-charmer, scavenger, merchant,
        mahout,
Each life in this land that is sore has the chance to soar
    To find and keep that friend. But, for myself, I doubt.

IV

The last light purples the mirrors of paddy, the tracks
Become dark rivers of peasants with brushwood on their heads,
Rivers which all day long flowed out of sight
Leaving the world to children. Now the palmtrees
Grow dark like gigantic fly-whisks and the church
A glimpse of white that might be a temple; though here
The lingam, could it be here, were only an axis
Abstracted from or imagined on space, while space
Shrinks to a granite hide-out and the world
Turns round that hollow kernel where all noise
Lies folded away like grave-clothes. Only a whisper
More tenuous than the shriek of one lost bat
Spins out like the one weak thread of one lost spider,
The ghost of the groping doubt of one lost man.

Thomas, Thomas, were you right
In your blindness to preach light?
Cowering there in that dark crypt
With body and soul so ill equipped
And the Christ whom once you knew
Torn for ever from your view,
Thomas, Thomas, do you find
That out of sight means out of mind?

Out of sight . . . These millions, where do they vanish in the
daytime?
These ants who thrust and haul the crumbs from Shiva's table
While Shiva's foot, as he dances, hangs above them,
Their life being merely between one step and the next,
One tap on the drum and the next. And the gospel of Thomas
Which grants each ant its worth is only by proxy
Since Thomas himself is a proxy, hawking a faith
That he knows should be theirs while he dare not assume it is
his
Unless he confirm and remind himself by his hands
Caressing his walls of rock, batting the flies,
Or pressing them merely together, those hands that once
Were tested and proved, yet failed through needing a test.

Thomas, Thomas, do you not
Even yet repent your lot?
Fisherman who left your boat
To trawl for souls, nameless, remote,
Which when you catch and lift them high
Flash like mackerel and then die.
What started this you know—but why?
Thomas, Thomas, do not lie!

Liar? Not Thomas; he had too much doubt
And hair on the back of his hands, they looked so clumsy
Yet in the dark could tell new twine from old
And tell himself himself, they had taught him once
That a spirit was still a man, since when in his sleep

42

More than awake they grope as if under sea
To prove all men are spirit. Believing Thomas,
Apostle to the Indies! If never there,
The Indies yet can show in a bare church
On a bare plaque the bare but adequate tribute
To one who had thrust his fingers into the wounds of God.

V

OUR SISTER WATER

I

World's best is water; in the megrims of parched
Towns where the sun's laugh drills into the occiput
Or in brown uplands where river beds parody
Bubbles with pebbles, rivers with rock.

Heart's best is water; behind the glaring
Stucco of faces, lost in wrinkles,
In clefts of rubbish and fluttering newspaper,
Might be a rivulet; heart's, world's best.

O my dear sister, my dear Sor Acqua,
Useful and humble and precious and chaste,
Might we, admiring no less than needing,
Name you not also spendthrift? Harlot?

Francis preached to the birds but Pindar
In a land still drier sung for the oligarchs,
Found no image to praise their virtue
Better than water, colourless, pure.

Yet, as we know, my wraith of the backstairs,
Underground whisperer, queen of mirage,
None has more ball-dresses, pheasant or kingfisher,
More golden armour, plate or chain.

Whose name was writ in . . . Keats was right;
They would wish on us hearts of oak, of iron,
Or even of gold—all crude things, tame,
To the wealth and whip and gamut of water.

Blind in the desert the palate shrills:
Wine is for luxury, milk for babes,
But for men dying water is all
To be wished. Is also the wish to live.

In gas, maybe, the world began
But in water we. Thales was right;
Stone can stand, steel thrust, but we
May dodge betwixt, may slither between;

Spinning our senses thin to diaphanous
Film over sand or marble slab,
Humping our passions in tidal waves,
Booming a cataract, tinkling a raindrop.

Water our core and water our trivia;
Here on this grid of cemented heat
We wilt at a table and order a Turkish
Coffee. To pay for. Water is free.

Water is free; she comes in a tumbler.
Coffee is charged for, comes in a cup,
A hot sweet thimbleful thick with grounds
But a tower of liquid light beside it

Which the sun coins and cool from ice
It spears the throat like an ice-cold sun.
The cup is a gulp of dregs; but double,
But triple our tumblers, turrets of water.

Sister! Look forth on the heat-crazed road;
Is that the sandstorm? Those dry daemonia,
Mark how they dance! But you, you can match them:
Jongleurs de Dieu, tumblers of God.

Back in the Seventeen-Seventies to Birmingham he came,
The Scot, John Watt, of combustion engine fame,
Having lived overlong in a hobside dream,
Murdering his sister Water, turning her to steam;
Then Watt, having got what he wanted most, her ghost,
Packed her off to Birmingham, his wee key post,
Where he and Matthew Boulton built a limbo dark and high
To blazon English locomotives black across the sky.

The great Soho foundry is there to this day;
From the thick black sand the red flames play,
The molten metal slops, trundled round by hand,
By the black hands on the barrows, in the thick black sand,
And a thick black laugh from a man you cannot see
Takes a pot shot at Watt and his point d'appui;
For Watt's soft spot was for things that puff and bray
But those rich red gutters make weighing machines today.

Now a metre of green being, as a Frenchman said,
Greener than a centimetre, if machines are dead
And a fortiori dry, the driest, deadest of the lot
Are these finicking machines which were not designed by Watt
And Watt may be turning, between disgust and rage,
In his grave which is the grave of the whole Steam Age,
Or else, all passion spent, may wink the other eye
From that grave which is so narrow, so dirty, so dry.

Water, Water, Watt! You dealt us mere steam;
Hard cash flowed but can dividends redeem
The desiccated banks, the clinker paths designed
To weld a mobile body to a bone-dry mind?
Water, water, Watt! You were never in the South,
A dour northern hero with a dry northern mouth,
And your name is writ in steam over heaven—perhaps a blot
Here and there—but, in my ear-drum, were you ever thirsty,
    Watt?

Steam is a dry word; the best word is water
For artist and peasant however the sewers debase it,
Whatever foul acid may slur it. Best in the West
Squelching round ankles, dousing the nape of the neck,
Ringing the jackpot of colour out of the mountains;
Best in the large or best when a girl in a shawl
Barefoot and windblown staggers her way through the bog
With a bucket of windblown gold. Best in the East
Where humpbacked oxen maunder down a ramp
To brim the pitchers of the girls in saris,
Or in flat plats of paddy sprigged with green,
Or on the rulered page of a Moghul garden—
Cool marrow of marble spines; or in the endless
Plains in the gross monsoon with one white egret
Posed on a stump among red miles of soup,
Red miles of wheat to be. In large or little
And east or west the best. As on these marches
Of East and West where beneath this capheneion table
Pistachio shells lie dry as fag-ends, poor pink shells
That never savoured brine; and in the street,
Where dust of down-coming houses irks the nostrils,
Red mouths of water melons gape and slobber
Red in a cart of great green globes while women,
Dark handkerchiefs over dark glasses over dark eyes,
Like inquisitorial puppets fidget past
Towards some dry catechism. Look at the melons,
You wire-drawn fates, and wait! As Stephenson and Watt
For an opposite cause waited and watched the kettle
Boil itself dry, dry. As the chosen people
Waited while Moses raised his rod to Yahweh
Through a second of dry eternity; then split it
Into a gash of silver. Or as we wait
Now for a coffee—and the more grounds the better
To prove that crystal crystal, that water wet,

Which will be slapped in free. Great things in little:
A leaf from Moses' rod, a psalm of David,
Trapped in a tumbler. Japanese flowers. A magnum
Of light in liquid. Stand on your heads you fountains,
Be lifted up you long horizontal lakes,
Spout your trombones of silver and you seas
Balloon your whales in the sky, make Pegasuses
Of all your white and randy horses. In Pindar's
Land his word runs true. Water is best:
A miracle out of the rock, a royal flush in the hand,
A river nymph on the table. Tumbler, chameleon,
Clown, conjuror of God!

IV

Water is beginning, is end, is pure, is pure gift
Of always shifting ground as never ground can shift,
In which being of which having weltered once, today
Soul retains what body lost scrambling out of a bay,
Shackling itself in legs: our birthright which we sold
For a mess of lungs and limbs. Even now we contain an untold
Capacity for sliding, rippling, filtering under the limestone hill,
Moving in order under ice, charging in combers, lying still,
Reflecting faces, refracting light, transparent or opaque,
Can be wind-curled fountain, tigerish weir, garrulous rain or
        tongue-tied lake,
Can be all shapes or shapeless, assume all voices or none,
Can alchemise rock and pavement, flatter and fleece the sun,
Maraud and mime and bless. Such is water, such are we,
World's most variables, constant in our variability,
Termagants and trulls of froth, virgins in the naked heart,
Bombardiers of breaker and bore, who in the end sidle apart
Into still cells of crystal. As Keats in the end withdrew
To Rome and his own illness, left his sister Water a new
Name for her silver archives, Adonais, the maiden knight

Of the sensual world; and his sister, veiled in white,
Wrote it and traces it still with her finger. Water and we are
    alive,
We talk and twist, fill out all moulds, contrive
Inroads into the alien, raiding the solid black
Preserves of earth or assaulting air, yet must fall back
In the end and find our level absolved of earth and breath
In that bed we were conceived in, born in, the bed of ocean, of
    death.

VI

THE ISLAND

I

First the distant cocks. A hairfine
Etching on silence, antiphonal silver,
Far-flung nooses of glittering sound,
   A capstan chanty to launch the day,
While the young though time-honoured Early Riser
   Fingers and proves her way.

Then the donkeys; clumsily splicing
Coarser hausers—Haul away, bullies,
For all your grumps and catarrh. Be docile,
   Enter those golden shafts and heave
The chariot over the mountain, freighted
   Once more with a reprieve.

Next and together a gush of water
And gabble of Greek. The sluices are open,
Each to his runnel, down from the mountain,
   From thriftily hoarded dams of sleep,
It flows as arranged; we are back to daylight
   When men and plants drink deep.

Back to normal; the ghosts in the pinetrees
Have dwindled to lizards; primaeval brows
Lined with a myriad drystone terraces
   Smile in the sun; the welded blue
Of sea and sky is the tenure of legend;
   Far; near; true.

Always begun so. Cutting his capers
On mattock and needle, sun on the cypresses
Polishing cone-studs as in Homeric
     Times when he brassed the boss on the shield
Of some rough-hewn hero under the cypresses
     And held out fame in the field.

But then, as now, Sun was deceiver
Who promised no more than he could give
But than men could take, dangling before them
     Wealth, glory, freedom, life;
When Icarus flew too high that freedom
     Lopped his wings like a knife

And he fell by this island. Where the woodsmoke
Smelt as now, where the naked rocks
Were as naked then, where labouring wisdom
     Then as now, ready to leave
Things till tomorrow, asked of tomorrow
     No freedom, only reprieve.

II

Which still is much. Here in this mountain village
Favoured with trees, bareness above and below it,
Suspended over a sea which melts in a sky suspended
Over a little blue dome which melts, which melts in upper
And nether blueness: here, one might think, is a closed
Circle, cave of Calypso. No horizon
Beyond the sombre warmth of looseknit stones, beyond
The warmth of daily greetings—no horizon
Did not these whitewashed rooms among wine-gourds, goat-
     skins, ikons,
Include a letter or two with a foreign postmark
From Cleveland and Detroit, diners and luncheonettes,

From wholesale grocers, coffee jobbers, gobetweens,
Who proved there was a horizon when they crossed it
Yet still are sons and uncles. Hermes came from Olympus
Tipster and god of the market; these across the Atlantic,
Tides invading the tideless. Where was the land of the dead
Rise now the towers of life, the steel and concrete
Which scorn yet prop these cabins. Hermes parted the creepers
That screened the cave of the nymph, gave her his ultimatum
And left. As the sun will leave who is peeping now through
    the figtree
But also broods on Wall Street. The epithets of Homer
Were fixed, albeit capricious, including the compounds
With God in them, by dint of repetition
Or ignorance ringing true. As cockcrow and cicada
Argue that light will last. The timeworn baker,
Burnt out of Smyrna, smokes his hubble-bubble,
The grey stones breathe in sky, a slim and silent girl
Gathers salt from the sea-crags, green among green leaves
Figs, kid-soft purses, bulge, on low stone roofs
Figs, grapes, tomatoes, dry in the sun and sweat
Pastes the hair to the forehead, a tall woman
Strides out of Homer over the pine-needles, mule-droppings,
Holding a distaff while the swallowtail butterflies
Fly, or seem to, backwards. Seem to. Backwards.
The sluices were all closed hours ago; where the water
Tumbled the rocks are dry, our shadows are short in the sun,
Painters would find this innocent. If difficult.
Its blue too blue. And giving nothing away.

III

Gorged on red, green, purple, tomatoes, peppers, aubergine,
    The visitor lies among tattered shadows
Under a walnut tree where a high sun shines through the
        smooth green

Leaves so unlike the leaves of Athens,
Those dusty rats' tails. An August siesta. Here, he feels, is
  peace,
The world is not after all a shambles

And, granted there is no God, there are gods at least, at least in
  Greece,
And begins to drowse; but his dreams are troubled
By the sawmill noise of cicadas, on and on—Will they never
  cease?

Were he to count a thousand, a hundred
Thousand sheep, they would all be scraggy and stare at him
  with the stare
Of refugees, outraged and sullen,

Who have no gap to go through, who even if free are free as
  air
Long since exhausted. And the cicadas
Force, force the pace; a jaunty cavalcade of despair.

Idyllic? Maybe. Still there is hardly
Such a thing as a just idyl. The sanguine visitor dreams
And finds himself on the run with barking

Dogs at his heels who turn into wolves, into men, and each of
  them seems
To be running in creaky shoes; before him
Brood vast grey rocks, turtle-shape, cottage-loaf, rubble of
  dried-up streams,

Among which reigns the judge in his glory
In a wig like a dirty sheep, frightened himself, with a nerve in
  his face
Ticking away, giving wisdom and warning

In the voice of a circular saw. Forcing the pace, forcing the
pace,
Did not a quick breeze scour the treeless
Dream and also the tree that shelters the dreamer, yet cannot
efface

The truth of his panic; these are no megrims,
This is the world and this island—a brown leaf clanks from the
green tree
Dry on dry ground like a subpoena—

And there are prisoners really, here in the hills, who would not
agree
To sign for their freedom, whether in doubt of
Such freedom or having forgotten or never having known what
it meant to be free.

IV

Our shadows now grow long in the sun,
Not to be long in it. No horizon
All day for the brightness of sea and sky,
All night for their darkness. One by one
The clefts are closed and the colours run
And the olive groves turn muted velvet.

Later the water. Through his contrived
Miniature channel he dives and prattles
To puddle the powdery grooves; his voice
Breaks where the steep from which he dived
Turns level; but the earth revived
Feels young this evening, as this morning.

59

Our shadows walk on stilts, look old
As our ambitions, the sun is younger
Having no dreams; like a self-made god
Who mouths his mottoes, parades his gold,
But swaggers off with the facts untold,
The name on his cheque still wet behind him.

The water-talk ends; the scrawl on the sky
Smudges and fades, the upper and nether
Darknesses close, the night grinds small,
Gives nothing away; but frail and high
A new moon rides and the starved eye
Finds the full circle in the crescent.

Finds or seems to. Seems to. A full
Circle and full close. One donkey
Erupts, a foghorn, then runs down
Like a worn disc; and the moon's pull
On these dark seas comes weak or null
As the will and whims of a jilted goddess.

That gods are grudged the loves of men
Born proof against a life immortal
Calypso knew before Hermes spoke;
She sleeps alone in her cave since then
While the tired peasants in this glen
Lie upon planks, at least together.

Some who lived long on this poor soil
No more have part in it; their twilight
Falls eight hours later, their evening meals
Like their morning minds are soon on the boil
But where is their island wine and oil?
Where the slow concord of an island?

Slow. As life is. One by one,
Islands themselves, the stars move forward
In echelon, in grave pursuit
Of a routed, already returning sun
Who seems to be falling back, on the run.
Seems to. Back. Yet marches forward.

The round of dark has a lip of light,
The dams of sleep are large with daybreak,
Sleeping cocks are primed to crow
While blood may hear, in ear's despite,
The sun's wheels turning in the night
Which drowns and feeds, reproves and heartens.

VII

DAY OF RENEWAL

I

Do I prefer to forget it? This middle stretch
Of life is bad for poets; a sombre view
Where neither works nor days look innocent
And both seem now too many, now too few.
They told me as a child that ten was a ripe age
When presents must be useful; which was Progress
But I felt sad to end each fairy story,
Kept turning back to the first page.

Candles increased, then vanished. Where I was born,
Heckled by hooters and trams, lay black to the west
And I disowned it, played a ticklish game
Claiming a different birthplace, a wild nest
Further, more truly, west, on a bare height
Where nothing need be useful and the breakers
Came and came but never made any progress
And children were reborn each night.

Go west and live. Not to become but be.
Still that remains an ideal—or a pretence;
Death is, but life becomes, and furthest westward
The dead must lap fresh blood to recover sense
As Homer rightly thought. Birthdays come round
And the child graduates from milk to meat
And loses count of himself, finding and losing
Visions as quickly lost as found.

As time, so place. This day a year ago
Or thirty years lies rooted in one spot
Which in itself has changed but in our mind
Does not become but is; is what it now is not.

Thus for me Cushendun is war and frustrated
Love, Dieppe an astringent idyl, Lahore
Blood, cholera, flies, blank eyes, becoming forty:
Each birthday placed and each place dated.

Such and such my beginnings, launched and engined
With such and such a tackle of nerve and gland
And steered by such and such taboos and values,
My What and How science might understand
But neither the first nor last page tells the story
And that I am remains just that I am.
The whole, though predetermined to a comma,
Still keeps its time, its place, its glory.

II

Turn again, Whittington. Riding the surf
Of the winds of England far-off bells
Change and taunt you, change and tempt you:
Turn again, Whittington, your pocket full of milestones.
And so for all of us. Fits and starts,
Bronze tongues lost in a breaking wave,
Then clear on the crest. When his grimy bundle
Bred vaults of gold and his cat was dead,
Still the bells rang the same. Same changes.
Same. Is life. Changes. Is life.
One-Two-Three-Four-Five-Six-Seven-Eight:
This year, no year, ever, never, next time,
Eat your cake, have your cake, last time lucky,
Ace high, bottoms up, cut again, turn again,
This year, next year, a pocket full of plumstones,
All the white horses and—turn again, Whittington—
All the King's aldermen sweating on the bellropes
Cannot put together again, by no means whatsoever again,
What time and tide have parted—brickbats and dividends.

Orange flotsam, lemon jetsam, Tower Reach is bobbing with it
And never put together again. Bow bells and coster carts.
I'm sure I don't, the bell says, the great bell, the tenor bell
Booming out of the brine trough, swinging on the world's
    wheel,
Mouth up in ribaldry, I'm sure I don't, an oracle
For lord mayors and beggar boys, I'm sure I don't know!

And so for all of us. Bits and pieces,
Mayoral banquet and barefoot mile,
Here the self-licensed purr of a cat
And there the toasts, the commercial phrases:
This year? Next year? When will you pay me?
Ever and always. Long may he live!
But the clappers overlap in the waves
And the words are lost on the wind. Five farthings . . .
Five farthings for what? For turtles? Candles?
The great procession comes once a year
Like Christmasses, birthdays. Gifts and leases;
They all run out. As a man's wardrobe
Bulges with clothes he no longer wears
Or only on off days; turned again,
Turned and returned, darned and patched,
Stained with memories. Moth and clock
Have done their damn'dest. Ancient brogues
Caught in a wrinkled grin when the wind changed
Repeat their inglenook yarns, remember
Only one walk out of many; a hat
With a bent black brim remembers a funeral;
And white drills drill in India. Memories
Flitter and champ in a dark cupboard
While in a box among old tin whistles
And paper caps lie stubs of candles
Twisted, snuffed out, still in their holders,
Relics of Christmas, birthday butts.

Ding! Dong! Pussy's in the ding-dong!
Who put us here? The daily why,
The birthday But. We are still children;
Don't Care was hung, Did Care was haunted;
Big A, Little A, Why's in the cupboard;
Why, say the children, is Why in the cupboard?
And what is that light at the top of the well?
Who'll pull us out? We want that light
At the top of the well. On my next birthday
Shall I get out? Or the one after next?
Or the next after that? Or the next after that?
Here come the candles; now can I do it?
The light up above us is one big candle.
To light us to what? To what, say the doubting
Children and stay but not for an answer.
Ding! Dong! What? Ding! Dong! Why?

III

Milestones. My own; small things lost in a vast
Forest of marble obelisks, private code-words
Drowned in a maelstrom of wavelengths. The lines are crossed;
The miles are a wrong number; the rivers are jammed
With angry logs on which in great spiked boots
Lumberjacks fight each other and when one falls
They stamp upon his face. While on the shore
The self withdraws to its third floor back, shakes out
Its fears, hopes, hungers, loves, its doubts and visions,
The small things that are its own; which tinkle, sparkle,
Then roll off into corners. What is own?
The corners maybe but the light they danced in
Came through the window, the same light that still
Gilds the murderous river, catches the spikes
On the boot that is raised to blind. So what is own?
One's birthday is a day that people die on—

Shorthand of wavering shadow on white icing
Scribbled by tiny candles. Thus for me
Being twenty-one was at home but seemed at large
For all the coming slump. And being thirty
Was London and the fear of growing old,
Also the fear of war. And being forty
Was an arm sore from the needle, a Tom Collins
In the garden of Faletti's with Lilac Time
Tinkling between the massacres, was Lahore
When all the lines were dead. And now I am forty-three,
At sea in the small hours heading west from the island
Where other massacres drove poor folk west
To make this Turkish delight, so soft and sweet
It lights up one's bad tooth. In the small dark hours
At sea this time and westwards—west to live
A small hour though my own. But next time? (What
Are those lights ahead? Already the port so loved
By Themistocles, great patriot and statesman,
Great traitor five years on?) But next time what?

IV

This year, last year, one time, ever,
Different, indifferent, careless, kind,
Ireland, England, New England, Greece—
The plumstones blossom in my mind.

A child inside me lights the beacons
Which spell both victory and defeat,
Candles that he cannot see
Around a cake he dare not eat.

Peasticks and dried pea-stalks and empty
Cartons, old letters and dead leaves;
My odd job conscience lights a bonfire
Which gasps and crackles, exults and grieves.

For all my years are based on autumn,
Blurred with blue smoke, charred by flame,
Thrusting burnt offerings on a god
Who cannot answer to his name.

And purged of flowers that shone before me
I find in roots beyond me, past
Or future, something that outlasts me
Through which a different I shall last.

Whitewash, pebbledash, beaverboard, brick,
Plane tree, neem tree, crabapple, pine,
Freehold, leasehold, trespasser, tenant,
All men's, no man's, thine, mine.

For no one person may found a city
As Cadmus knew who, bowed beneath
His lonely burden, prayed for helpers,
Then cashed that bond of dragon's teeth.

Born as we are in need of friends
We take our fears and sow the earth
Which burgeons with them, fully grown,
Too many for comfort, armed from birth.

Mentor, tempter, mistress, wife,
Helping, hampering, casual, dear,
Every dark furrow sprouts with eyes
And from each eye there shines a spear.

Hence mutual clashes where some fall,
None but a few survive to lay
The needed stones and light the fires
Which make and unmake every day.

To eat one's cake and have it? Perhaps
In the end we can; when no one flame
Shines less than all and through blown smoke
There drifts a god who needs no name.

VIII

DAY OF RETURNING

I

Crouched upon sea-chiselled gravel, staring out and up at the
    sea,
  The gnarled and glorious twister, seasoned in danger, wept,
Thrusting his heart at that monstrous wall of water
  Beyond which somewhere was Ithaca.

Behind him the island was terraced, before him terrace on
    terrace of waves
  Climbed to the cruel horizon; though he was strong, he
    wept,
The salt tears blent and blurred with the salt spindrift
  While the salt of his wit grew savourless.

Behind him also, faintly curling out of the woods, a voice,
  Which once entranced, now pained him; instead of that too
    sweet song
He yearned for the crisp commands of laundry and kitchen
  Which his wife must be giving in Ithaca.

And again he rode his mind at the hurdles of ocean, counted the
    hours
  That would not pass, the waves that would not sleep, and
    wept
But not as of old when he half enjoyed the weeping
  For shared sorrows in company.

But this was not tragic, this was frustration; infertile as the foam
  That creamed around his sandals, listless as the hope
The sweet voice held out sometimes of an immortal
  Life, but life here, not Ithaca.

For here his bed was too soft and the wine never rough and the
    scent of the flowers
  Too heavy; here when he should have smiled he wept.
Better have stayed on that other island of lotus
  Smiling from pure forgetfulness.

Out and up at the sea. A stiff climb for a tired mind
  And nothing at the top; the terraces dissolved
In the clambering eye; while a voice sang on, destroying
  All heart, all hope, all Ithaca.

II

Home beyond this life? Or through it? If through, how?
Through as through glass—or through the nerves and blood?
We all are homeless sometimes, homesick sometimes,
As we all at times are godless or god-fearing—
  And what does that imply?

On scrubbed white deal two hands, red from the sink, are
    clenched
On the hope of an after-life; there is dirt in the cracks
Of the table and under the nails for all their scouring
And the golden walls of Jerusalem the Golden
  Have black cracks in them too.

Zion is always future. Just as Calypso's isle
Was always and too present, so out of time;
But home is seen and lived through time, the alarm clock
Rules from the kitchen shelf and the dog Argus
  Grows old and vexed with fleas.

On Sundays perhaps the alarm is stilled and the red hands
Reposed on a Sunday lap in the just-so room
Which does not exist on weekdays, where the Penates

Are no more jug nor clock but family photos
    Of a family not to the life.

Stiff collars and a harmonium. White and black. Stiff keys.
A creaking lock in gates of mother of pearl.
The street is curtained off that up and inwards
The mind may count the golden rungs, though Jacob
    Unseen limp down the street.

A stiff climb—and at the top? Will Wesley hand us a gold
Chalice of nectar—immortal and islanded life,
A home from home? But is it a window or mirror
We see that happiness in or through? Or is it
    Merely escape from the clock?

As Penelope never escaped. And, though her husband did,
He found that bliss a prison and each day
Wept as he watched the changing unchanging ocean
Beyond which lived his wife and the dog Argus
    And real people. Who lived.

III

But even so, he said, daily I hanker, daily
Ache to get back to my home, to see my day of returning
After those years of violent action—and these of inaction.
Always and even so. But I have no ship, no comrades,
Only my wits with nothing to grind on. Nectar, ambrosia,
Promise me nothing; the goddess no longer pleases me.
Who would be loved by a goddess for long? Hours which are
    golden
But unreal hours, flowers which forget to fall,
And wine too smooth, no wrinkles to match my own—
Who would be loved by a goddess who cannot appreciate
The joy of solving a problem, who never wept

For friends that she used to laugh with? I stare at the sea
Till that hard horizon rounds one great round eye
Hard as that of the Cyclops; this time I have no
Means of putting it out—and now I am really No Man
For my ears ring with a too sweet voice which never
Falters or ages. They call me crafty Odysseus;
I have used my craft on gods and nymphs and demigods
But it is time, high time, I turned it again
To the earth that bred it, a new threshing floor
Or setting up boundary stones, for even the best
Neighbours encroach—and I like to have someone to argue
    with
About my rights of grazing or wood-cutting; aye, it is time
I heard the bleat of my goats and smelt the dung of my cattle;
Here there is neither dung nor rights nor argument,
Only the scent of flowers and a too sweet voice which is ever
Youthful and fails to move me. Here could never be home,
No more than the sea around it. And even the sea
Is a different sea round Ithaca.

IV

They call me crafty, I robbed my brother,
Hoaxed my father, I am most practical,
Yet in my time have had my visions,
Have seen a ladder that reached the sky.
A smooth old man but when I was younger—
You noticed my limp, here, in the thigh—
I wrestled all night with God Eternal.

Which one can never do twice. And the ladder
I never saw that again either; presumably
It is there always if one could see it
And the shining messengers, busy as bees,

78

Go up and come down it searching for honey
In the hearts of men; they are hard to please,
Want only the best. But we know when they find it

Because we feel suddenly happy. For all that
One should not think too much about them; analysis
Cannot hit off what they want; it is better
To keep one's eyes on the earth and they
Can take their tithes when they choose, they are welcome,
But now is my home and here is my day
And my job is to father a chosen people.

A hard job but grateful. Laban exacted
Seven years of diligent bailiffry,
Then tried to cheat me; my wives, my children,
Proved jealous; followed the years of dearth
When Joseph was lost—but God had assured me
My seed should be as the dust of the earth
And Joseph and corn were found in Egypt.

Yet sometimes, even now, I have a nightmare,
Always the same, that the challenge has come again
In a stony place, in ultimate darkness,
And I feel my sinews crack in advance
And, because this time I know my opponent,
I know that this time I have no chance
Of holding my own. My own is nowhere;

And I wake in a sweat, still in the darkness
Which might be nowhere—but I am most practical,
I put out my hand to finger the darkness
And feel the nap of it, it is my own,
Enclosed by myself with walls and enclosing
My family; besides, the ache in the bone
Of my thigh confirms me that I am somewhere,

That I am home; no more a vagrant,
No more—except in flashes—a visionary,
No more a chooser, I have been chosen
To father the chosen, a full time task—
With by-products perhaps such as shall we say honey—
Still on the whole I have little to ask
But that day should return, each day of returning.

IX

THE DEATH OF A CAT

I

Since then, those months ago, these rooms miss something,
A link, a spark, and the street down there reproves
My negligence, particularly the gap
For the new block which, though the pile of timber
Is cleared on which he was laid to die, remains
A gap, a catch in the throat, a missing number.

You were away when I lost him, he had been absent
Six nights, two dead, which I had not learnt until
You returned and asked and found how he had come back
To a closed door having scoured the void of Athens
For who knows what and at length, more than unwell
Came back and less than himself, his life in tatters.

Since when I dislike that gap in the street and that obdurate
Dumb door of iron and glass and I resent
This bland blank room like a doctor's consulting room
With its too many exits, all of glass and frosted,
Through which he lurked and fizzed, a warm retort,
Found room for his bag of capers, his bubbling flasket.

For he was our puck, our miniature lar, he fluttered
Our dovecot of visiting cards, he flicked them askew,
The joker among them who made a full house. As you said,
He was a fine cat. Though how strange to have, as you said
     later,
Such a personal sense of loss. And looking aside
You said, but unconvincingly: What does it matter?

To begin with he was a beautiful object:
Blue crisp fur with a white collar,
Paws of white velvet, springs of steel,
A Pharaoh's profile, a Krishna's grace,
Tail like a questionmark at a masthead
And eyes dug out of a mine, not the dark
Clouded tarns of a dog's, but cat's eyes—
Light in a rock crystal, light distilled
Before his time and ours, before cats were tame.

To continue, he was alive and young,
A dancer, incurably male, a clown,
With his gags, his mudras, his entrechats,
His triple bends and his double takes,
Firm as a Rameses in African wonderstone,
Fluid as Krishna chasing the milkmaids,
Who hid under carpets and nibbled at olives,
Attacker of ankles, nonesuch of nonsense,
Indolent, impudent, cat catalytic.

To continue further: if not a person
More than a cypher, if not affectionate
More than indifferent, if not volitive
More than automaton, if not self-conscious
More than mere conscious, if not useful
More than a parasite, if allegorical
More than heraldic, if man-conditioned
More than a gadget, if perhaps a symbol
More than a symbol, if somewhat a proxy
More than a stand-in—was what he was!
A self-contained life, was what he must be
And is not now: more than an object.

And is not now. Spreadeagled on coverlets—

Those are the coverlets, bouncing on chairbacks—
These are the chairs, pirouetting and sidestepping,
Feinting and jabbing, breaking a picture frame—
Here is the picture, tartar and sybarite,
One minute quicksilver, next minute butterballs,
Precise as a fencer, lax as an odalisque,
And in his eyes the light from the mines
One minute flickering, steady the next,
Lulled to a glow or blown to a blaze,
But always the light that was locked in the stone
Before his time and ours; at best semi-precious
All stones of that kind yet, if not precious,
Are more than stones, beautiful objects
But more than objects. While there is light in them.

III

Canyons of angry sound, catastrophe, cataclysm,
Smells and sounds in cataracts, cat-Athens,
Not, not the Athens we know, each whisker buzzing
Like a whole Radar station, typhoons of grapeshot,
Crossfire from every roof of ultra-violet arrows
And in every gutter landmines, infra-red,
A massed barrage of too many things unknown
On too many too quick senses (cossetted senses
Of one as spoilt as Pangur Ban, Old Foss
Or My Cat Jeoffrey), all the drab and daily
Things to him deadly, all the blunt things sharp,
The paving stones a sword dance. Chanting hawkers
Whose street cries consecrate their loaves and fishes
And huge black chessmen carved out of old priests
And steatopygous boys, they all were Gogs and Magogs
With seven-league battering boots and hair-on-ending voices
Through which he had to dodge. And all the wheels

85

Of all the jeeps, trucks, trams, motor-bicycles, buses, sports
    cars,
Caught in his brain and ravelled out his being
To one high horrible twang of breaking catgut,
A swastika of lightning. Such was Athens
To this one indoors cat, searching for what
He could not grasp through what he could not bear,
Dragged to and fro by unseen breakers, broken
At last by something sudden; then dragged back
By his own obstinate instinct, a long dark thread
Like Ariadne's ball of wool in the labyrinth
Not now what he had played with as a kitten
But spun from his own catsoul, which he followed
Now that the minotaur of machines and men
Had gored him, followed it slowly, slowly, until
It snapped a few yards short of a closed door,
Of home, and he lay on his side like a fish on the pavement
While the ball of wool rolled back and down the hill,
His purpose gone, only his pain remaining
Which, even if purpose is too human a word,
Was not too human a pain for a dying cat.

IV

Out of proportion? Why, almost certainly.
You and I, darling, knew no better
Than to feel worse for it. As one feels worse
When a tree is cut down, an ear-ring lost,
A week-end ended, a child at nurse
Weaned. Which are also out of proportion.

Sentimentality? Yes, it is possible;
You and I, darling, are not above knowing
The tears of the semi-, less precious things,

A pathetic fallacy perhaps, as the man
Who gave his marble victory wings
Was the dupe—who knows—of sentimentality,

Not really classic. The Greek Anthology
Laments its pets (like you and me, darling),
Even its grasshoppers; dead dogs bark
On the roads of Hades where poets hung
Their tiny lanterns to ease the dark.
Those poets were late though. Not really classical.

Yet more than an object? Why, most certainly.
You and I, darling, know that sonatas
Are more than sound and that green grass
Is more than grass or green, which is why
Each of our moments as they pass
Is of some moment; more than an object.

So this is an epitaph, not for calamitous
Loss but for loss; this was a person
In a small way who had touched our lives
With a whisk of delight, like a snatch of a tune
From which one whole day's mood derives.
For you and me, darling, this is an epitaph.

X

FLOWERS IN THE INTERVAL

I

With you, pray not without you, trapped on the edge of the
    world
In the wind that troubles the galaxies, you my galactic
Marvel of ivoried warmth, with your warm hair curled
Over the cool of your forehead and your ambivalent
Tigercat eyes, which are amber and javelins, how,
How, my heart, did I dare to contrive this heartfelt
Artifice? Nonetheless, please take it now.

Without you once, in the wilderness, pondering years and
    years,
I heard thin strings in the air, came round a corner
On a quickset hedge of fiddlebows and my ears
Tingled because I was thinking of someone unknown to me
Who had pricked her finger and slept while the long nights
    grew
Into a tangle of quivering hands and gracenotes
Through which I plunged and found her—and she was you.

You, not anyone else; and your castle still stands there
But the thorns have blossomed, a young sun shines on the
    trumpets
And now there are rights of way since you have now made rare
Things common and very clean, a kind sun shines on the
    cabbage-plot
While a gay wind plays on the wheat, the plains are pearled
With dew and the willows are silver in wind—Can it possibly
Be the same wind that harries the ends of the world?

But to turn in on the world, you are all the places
That I have been in with you, blacked-out London,
Polperro's blue braided with gulls or Nephin
Striding beside us always on the right
While we were trudging west, you are the Tessin
Fuddled with oleanders, you are the crystal
Of the Venus Pool in Sark, you are Ménerbes
Anchored over the Midi, you are the comfort
Of Constable's mill in Suffolk, you are the miles
On miles of silence down Magilligan strand,
You are Marseilles on New Year's Eve with bottles
Parked at the crossings, you are the trolls' white limbs
Of Norway shagged with pineblack, you are the gentle
Green Stone Age forts of Dorset, and you are Greece
Armoured in Bronze Age light, you are Mycenae—
A gold mask in the darkness, you are the islands
With cyclamens and sheep bells or with the first
Flame of a single leaf on each black vine,
You are the folds of Hymettus, you are Delphi
(Eagle-colliding centre of the world)
Her ancient olives twisted into questions
Beneath the dead gymnasium, you are the air
Through which you flew to what was once Byzantium
Once Greek and once The City where un-Greek mists
Convey on belts across the Golden Horn
Cloth caps that fit poor Moslems, where Moslem domes
Rival the Holy Wisdom's, Moslem gravestones
Tilted like drunken chessmen still dare hint
At male and female forms, you are all these,
All these places. But also all the places
Where you have been without me; you are the Alps
Which crowned your early birthdays, you are Berlin
In ominous carnival, you are all the times
And places you were without me.

                    But still you,
In your own right and light; not anyone else.
For which, without or with me, I am grateful—
Without me yes, with me more yes. Because . . .

III

Because you intoxicate like all the drinks
We have drunk together from Achill Island to Athens,
Retsina or Nostrano, pops and clinks

Through snow or mist or mistral, aquavit
Or Château Neuf du Pape, from coloured inks
To the blood of bulls or sun-gods, dry or sweet,

Bitter or mild, armagnac, ouzo, stout,
Because, like each of these, you reprieve, repeat
Whether dry or sweet your newness, with or without

Water, and each one ray of you distils
A benediction and an end to doubt
Because your presence is all rays and rills;

Because your presence is baths of freesias, because
Your eyes are the gold-flecked loughs of Irish hills,
Your hands are Parvati and Millamant and what was

The earliest corn-and-fire dance is your hair,
Your stance is a caryatid's who seems to pause
Before she slips off, blandly unaware

Of the architrave on her head, because your moods
Are sun and water and because the air
Is burnished by you and the multitudes

Of humble moments answer to your voice
Like goldfish to a bell or sleeping woods
To a fresh breeze, because you make no choice

Unless you feel it first, because your laugh
Is Catherine wheels and dolphins, because Rejoice
Is etched upon your eyes, because the chaff

Of dead wit flies before you and the froth
Of false convention with it, because you are half
Night and half day, both woven in one cloth,

Because your colours are onyx and cantaloupe,
Wet seaweed, lizard, lilac, tiger-moth
And olive groves and beech-woods, because you scoop

The sun up in your hands, because your form
Is bevelled hills which neither crane nor stoop,
Because your voice is carved of jade yet warm

And always is itself and always new,
A pocket of calm air amidst a storm
And yet a ripple beneath all calms, a view

Into wide space which still is near; is you.

IV

In still grey dawn a delicate tendril
Climbs through the stillness, turns to song
And edging, dodging, through the grey,
Curling along, around, along,
Drops jasmine petals on the day
And adds one glint, one lift, to sunrise.

And so your voice. Through which forgotten
Ladies in wimple, ruff or hoop,
Bonnet or bustle, take the air
To join the shawled and kerchiefed troop
Of milkmaid, negress, vivandière,
Who sing when you sing, move as you do.

Of whom, thus launched, one rocks a firelit
Cradle beside a dying fire,
One wanders moonstruck on the fells,
One flirts and yields behind the byre,
And one, too proud to yield, repels
The taffeta phrases of her lover.

Thus Villon, Sidney, Campion, Purcell,
And all the unschooled anonymous Folk
Stand close behind you while you sing,
Restored by what their songs evoke
Through you and your interpreting,
Through you, your voice, your stance, your gesture.

So there you are, on a stage in a spotlight,
As here, on the edge of the world at home,
Making the absent present, awake
To the little voices of chalk and loam,
The lost tunes in the lonely lake
And the sunlit ghosts, receiving, giving.

Thus, when once more I round the corner,
I know your castle is also mine
And I know your dream defies the sands
Which count the minutes, I know the sign
That must let me in where your hair and hands
Are gay with the dawn, a waking beauty.

Like a walking dream. Like the first blossom,
Like a river fed from melting snow,
Like a leopardess with her cubs, like a bird
Returned from a land I did not know
Making unheard-of meanings heard
And sprinkling all my days with daylight.

And thus when the winds begin to whisper
Which lurk in the night and trouble space
I cross my fingers, grit my teeth,
And wait for the moment when your face
Appears from nowhere, as beneath
The frozen earth the bulbs burn upward.

The weathercock on the grey turret
Stirs in his sleep, the hedge of hands
Throws forth allegros in the sun
Which gilds and thwarts the dribbling sands
And green chords bind the barbican
While music tinkles from the hour-glass.

For you are there, are here, and nothing
Dare cancel that; you are my dear
With whom, pray not without, I live,
Incredibly ever-newly here
Each passing moment while you give
A timeless perfume to each moment.